Practice

Phonics

Louis Fidge

Hachette UK's policy is to use papers that are natural, renewable and recyclable products and made from wood grown in sustainable forests. The logging and manufacturing processes are expected to conform to the environmental regulations of the country of origin.

Orders: please contact Bookpoint Ltd, 130 Milton Park, Abingdon, Oxon OX14 4SB. Telephone: (44) 01235 827720. Fax: (44) 01235 400454. Lines are open 9.00a.m.–5.00p.m., Monday to Saturday, with a 24-hour message answering service. Visit our website at www.hoddereducation.co.uk.

© Louis Fidge 2013
First published in 2007 exclusively for WHSmith by
Hodder Education
An Hachette UK Company
338 Euston Road
London NW1 3BH

This second edition first published in 2013 exclusively for WHSmith by Hodder Education.
Teacher's tips © Najoud Ensaff 2013

Impression number   10 9 8 7 6 5 4 3 2 1
Year   2018 2017 2016 2015 2014 2013

Cover illustration by Oxford Designers and Illustrators Ltd
Character illustrations by Beehive Illustration
All other illustrations Fakenham Prepress Solutions, Fakenham, Norfolk NR21 8NN
Typeset in 16pt Folio by Fakenham Prepress Solutions, Fakenham, Norfolk NR21 8NN
Printed in Italy

A catalogue record for this title is available from the British Library.

ISBN: 978 1444 188 042

Age 5–7
Years 1–2
Key Stage 1

Advice for parents

This book is designed for children to complete on their own, but you may like to work with them for the first few pages.

- Don't get your child to do too much at once. A 'little and often' approach is a good way to start.

- Your child should work through the book unit by unit.

- Reward your child with lots of praise and encouragement.

- Talk to your child about what they have learnt and what they can do.

- The 'Get ready' section provides a gentle warm-up for the topic covered on the page.

- The 'Let's practise' section consolidates understanding of the topic. The questions in this section get progressively harder.

- The 'How have I done?' section is a short informal test that should be attempted when all the units have been completed. It is useful for spotting any gaps in knowledge, which can then be revisited at a suitable moment.

- The 'Teacher's tips' are written by practising classroom teachers. They give useful advice on specific topics or skills, to deepen your child's understanding and confidence and to help you help your child.

Phonics

Learning to read must be the single most important skill your child will learn at school. The way reading is taught has differed over the years, but recent research has shown the importance of giving young children a systematic programme of phonic work.

Phonics is a method of teaching reading by matching the letters of the alphabet to the sounds they make.

Learning these sounds, and how they form together as words, gives the early reader the tools they need to succeed.

With a sound phonic knowledge, your child will be able to 'sound out' unfamiliar words rather than rely on other clues such as pictures.

As reading ability increases then so should the ability to write. The spelling of words improves as your child becomes more confident in the use of letters.

Helping your child practise phonics at home is certainly time well spent. This book has been written to help you do just that. It covers the key areas of phonics that are taught in schools in England and Wales. It includes many of the common words that all children are expected to be able to read and write by the end of Year 2.

Contents

Welcome to Kids Club!

Hi, readers. My name's Charlie and I run Kids Club with my friend Abbie. Kids Club is an after-school club that is very similar to one somewhere near you.

We'd love you to come and join our club and see what we get up to!

I'm Abbie and I run Kids Club with Charlie. Let's meet the children who will work with you on the activities in this book.

My name is Jamelia. I look forward to Kids Club every day. There is always fun to be had with the activities we do. The sports and games are my favourites.

Hi, I'm Megan. I've made friends with all the children at Kids Club. I like the outings and trips we go on the best.

Hello, my name's Kim. Kids Club is a great place to chill out after school. My best friend is Alfie. He's a bit naughty but he means well!

I'm Amina. I like to do my homework at Kids Club. Charlie and Abbie are always very helpful. We're like one big happy family.

Greetings, readers. My name's Alfie! Everybody knows me here. Come and join our club. We'll have a wicked time together!

Now you've met us all, tell us something about yourself. All the children filled in a '**Personal Profile**' when they joined. There's one on the next page for you to complete.

Personal Profile

Name: _Oakley_ _____

Age: _____

School: _____

Home town: _____

Pets: _____

My favourite:

● book is _____,

● film is _____,

● food is _____,

● sport is _____.

My hero is _____ because _____

_____.

When I grow up, I want to be a _____.

If I could be king or queen for the day, the first thing I would do is _____

_____.

If I could be any animal for a day, I would be a _____

_____.

1: Word-building

We're making an alphabet snake. Charlie says the main **vowels** are *a*, *e*, *i*, *o*, *u* and that most words have at least one vowel in them. Now we're going to use the vowels to make some words. Can you help?

Get ready

①

c + a + t

cat

②

r + e + d

_____

③

p + i + n

_____

④

f + o + x

_____

⑤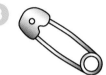

m + u + g

_____

⑥

t + i + n

_____

⑦

j + u + g

_____

⑧

b + e + d

_____

⑨

h + a + t

_____

⑩

b + o + x

_____

a b c d e f g m l k j i h n o p q r s t u v w x y z

Let's practise

Fill in the missing vowels.
Write the words that rhyme.

  a h_t on a r_t _____ _____

  a t_d on a b_d _____ _____

  a t_n on a b_n _____ _____

 a d_g on a l_g _____ _____

  a m_g on a r_g _____ _____

Write two words with the following endings:

an   **eg**   **ip**   **ot**   **un**

16 _____ _____ _____ _____ _____

_____ _____ _____ _____ _____

Read the words you wrote. Do they rhyme?

2: The *ch*, *sh* and *th* sounds

Abbie says that sometimes two letters come together and make one sound. Today we're saying the sounds **ch**, **sh** and **th**. Read these words with us and hear the sounds **ch**, **sh** and **th** in them.

chips   **sh**ip   mo**th**

Get ready

Complete the words. Write the words.

1

ch   <u>ch</u> at   ___in   ___op   ___ick

    <u>chat</u>   _____   _____   _____

2

sh   ___op   ___ed   ___ut   ___ell

    _____   _____ _____   _____

3

th   ___in   ___ick   ___ink   ___ank

    _____   _____   _____   _____

Now read all the words you made.

Let's practise

Complete the words with **ch**, **sh** or **th**. Write the words.

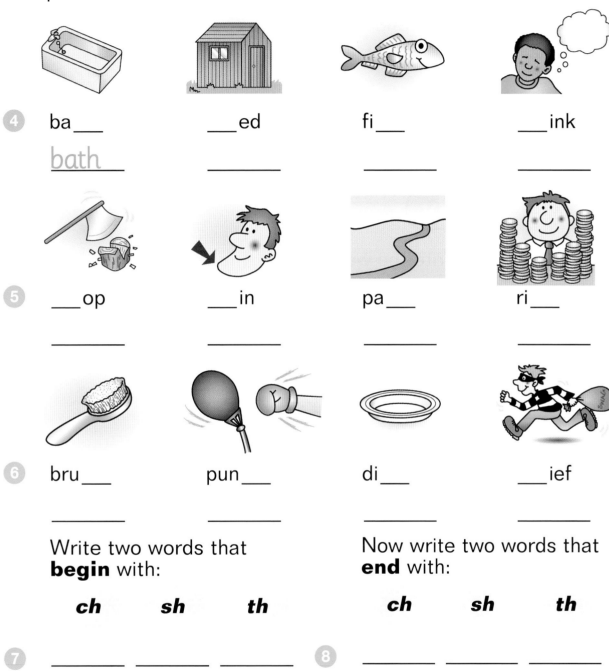

4   ba ___   ___ed   fi ___   ___ink

    bath   _____   _____   _____

5   ___op   ___in   pa ___   ri ___

    _____   _____   _____   _____

6   bru ___   pun ___   di ___   ___ief

    _____   _____   _____   _____

Write two words that **begin** with:

    ch   **sh**   **th**

7   _____ _____ _____

    _____ _____ _____

Now write two words that **end** with:

    ch   **sh**   **th**

8   _____ _____ _____

    _____ _____ _____

Teacher's tips

For question 7, remember you can use some of the words that have come up before, or maybe you can think of some of your own!

I'm collecting words ending with **ck**, **ng** or **ll**. When these letters come together they make one sound. Let's read some words and listen for the sounds.

du**ck**   ri**ng**   hi**ll**

Get ready

Make the words. Write the words. Read the words.

1   s | o | ck   k | i | ng   b | e | ll

sock   _____   _____

2   d | o | ll   t | i | ck   b | a | ng

_____   _____   _____

Label the pictures.

3

king   _____   _____

      ✓

_____   _____   _____

Let's practise

Read the words. Choose the correct word for each sentence.

| shell | wall | sing | king | rock | clock |

④

I fall off the _wall_ .

The _____ is on a swing.

⑤

A sock is on a _____ .

There is a bell on my _____ .

⑥

I can _____ a song.

The sock is on the _____ .

Read the words in the wall.

Colour the **ck** words red. Colour the **ng** words blue. Colour the **ll** words green.

⑦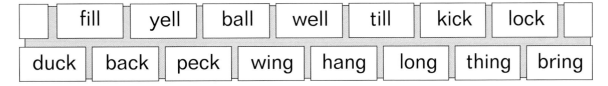

| | fill | yell | ball | well | till | kick | lock | |

| duck | back | peck | wing | hang | long | thing | bring |

Teacher's tips

For the *Let's practise* questions, notice that the underlined word in each sentence rhymes with another in the sentence. Use this and the pictures to help you fill in the spaces.

4: The *ee* and *ea* sounds

Today Charlie put up a sign. It said, 'S**ee** if you can r**ea**d this'. Of course, we all could! Then he said, 'Now look at how the letters **ee** and **ea** sometimes make the same sound.'

Can you read these words and hear the sounds?

I climb a tr**ee**.

I swim in the s**ea**.

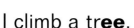
Get ready

Complete each word with **ee**.

1. b ee   sh___p   n___d

2. thr___   gr_____n w___k

Complete each word with **ea**.

3. ___t   r___d   b___ch

4. s___   sp___k   cl___n

Now read the words.

Underline the **ee** and **ea** words in the sentences.

I can <u>see</u> a <u>seal</u> in the <u>sea</u>. in the tree.

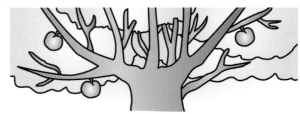

There are three green apples

I eat an ice cream on the beach.

I need to go to sleep!

I sit on a seat and read a book.

I sweep my room and make it clean.

Make a list of the **ee** words. Make another list of the **ea** words.

Complete each word correctly. Use **ee** or **ea**.

8   w__p   m__l   t__ch   st__p   k__p   n__t

      b__k   p__p   f__l   m__n   __ch   ch__k

Teacher's tips

If you need some help with question 8, ask a grown-up or see if any of the words have come up in any of your reading books. This might help you spell them correctly.

5: The *ay*, *ai* and *a-e* sounds

At Kids Club today, we're looking at the letters **ay**, **ai** and **a-e**. Sometimes they all make the same sound.

Can you read these words and listen to the sounds?

tr**ay**   r**ai**n   c**ak**e

Get ready

Complete the words. Notice that **ay** comes at the end of each word.

1

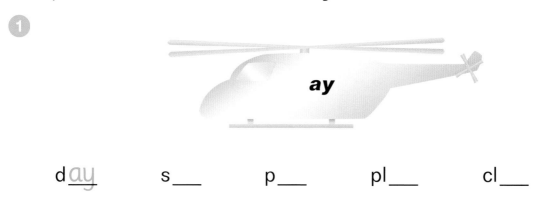

d ay   s ___   p ___   pl ___   cl ___

Complete the words. Notice that **ai** never comes at the end of a word.

2

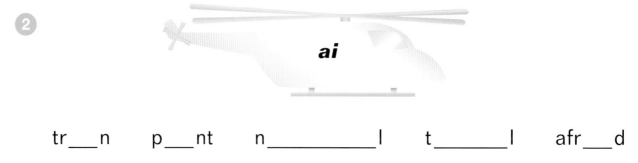

tr ___ n   p ___ nt   n _____ l   t _____ l   afr ___ d

Now read all the words you made.

Let's practise

Read these sentences from my diary. Complete the words with **ay** or **ai**.

③ On Sund__ay__ I went out to pl__ay__.

④  On Mond___ I went on a boat with a s___l.

⑤ On Tuesd___ I made a pot with cl___.

⑥ On Wednesd___ I saw a rat with a long t___l.

⑦ On Thursd___ I went for a swim in the b___.

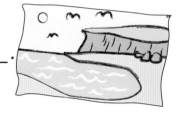

⑧ On Frid___ I got a hammer and hit a n___l.

Read these words. Add **e** to the end of each word. Read the new words. The vowel in the middle now makes a **long** sound!

hat   cap   mad   tap   can

Teacher's tips

A long 'a' sound is like the sound of the letter name: 'a'. The word *gate* has a long 'a' sound in it.

6: The *y*, *igh* and *i-e* sounds

Charlie told us the letters **y**, **igh** and **i-e** sometimes make the same sound.

A k**i**t**e** is h**igh** in the sk**y**.

Get ready

Make the words. Write the words. Read the words.

1

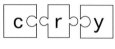
__cry__

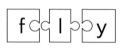
_____

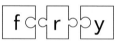
_____

Label the pictures.

2

__fry__

_____

_____

Make the words. Write the words. Read the words.

3

__light__

n c igh t
_____

f c igh t
_____

Let's practise

Find the **y** and *igh* words. Underline them.
Write the words. Read the words you
have written.

4

a	b	c	d	t	r	y	f	g	h
z	t	i	g	h	t	c	v	b	n
p	s	h	y	r	w	q	s	a	z
d	t	e	r	i	g	h	t	f	s
v	b	r	t	w	q	p	d	r	y
c	s	w	m	i	g	h	t	z	x
s	i	g	h	t	y	t	r	w	c
b	v	c	x	z	w	h	y	k	p
t	y	r	p	b	r	i	g	h	t

try
_____
_____
_____
_____
_____
_____
_____
_____

Read these words. Cross off the **e** at the end of each word.
Read the new words. The vowel in the middle now makes a
short sound!

5   pipe   ripe   wine   pine   spine

Teacher's tips

A short 'i' sound is like the sound in the word *bin*. A long 'i' sound is like the name of
the letter: i. There is a long 'i' in the word *time*.

17

I'm looking at the letters **ow**, **oa** and **o-e**.
Sometimes they make the same sound.
Let's read some of these words together.

sn**ow**   b**oa**t   b**o**ne

Get ready

Complete the words. Notice that **ow** comes at the end of each word.

1

l<u>ow</u>   bl___   sl___   sh___   gr___

Complete the words. Notice that **oa** never comes at the end of a word.

2

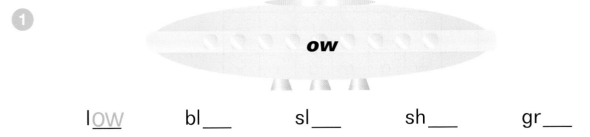

c___t   r_____d   l___f   s___p   m___n

Now read all the words you made.

Make some new words. Write the new words you make. Read the words.

3   Change the **l** to **m** in **l**ow.   _mow_

4   Change the **bl** to **sl** in **bl**ow.   _____

5   Change the **sn** to **sh** in **sn**ow.   _____

6   Change the **gr** to **cr** in **gr**ow.   _____

7   Change the **wind** to **shad** in **wind**ow.   _____

Complete each word with **oa**. Join the pairs of words that rhyme. Write the rhyming words. Read the words.

8   b__t   gr__n   _____

9   cl__k   g__t   _boat goat_

10   m__n   r__st   _____

11   r__d   s__k   _____

12   t__st   t__d   _____

Read these words. Add **e** to the end of each word. Read the new words. The vowel in the middle now makes a **long** sound!

13   hop   rob   not   slop   mop

Teacher's tips

A short 'o' sound is like the sound in the word *pot*. A long 'o' sound is like the name of the letter: o. There is a long 'o' in the word *rope*.

It was raining today, so I wore my new boots to Kids Club. They are blue – my favourite colour!

Charlie told us about the **oo, ew** and **u-e** letters. They sometimes make the same sounds.

Read the sentence he showed us. Listen to the sounds.

My n**ew** b**oo**ts are bl**ue**.

Get ready

Complete each word with **oo**. Now read the words.

1. z<u>oo</u>   p__l   r__f
2. m__n   b__t   r__m

Complete each word with **ew**. Now read the words.

3. n___   f__   ch___
4. st___   dr___   fl___

Let's practise

Complete each word with **oo** or **ew**.

5 m<u>oo</u>n   n___   ch___   b_t   br___m

6 st___   scr_____   sch___l   st___l   thr___

Now write the correct word under each picture.

7

threw   _____   _____   _____   _____

8

_____   _____   _____   _____   _____

Read these words. Cross off the **e** at the end of each word.
Read the new words. The vowel in the middle now makes a
short sound!

9 cube   use   tube   cute   plume

Teacher's tips

A short 'u' sound is like the sound in the word *rub*. A long 'u' sound is like the name
of the letter: u. There is a long 'u' in the word *fume*.

21

Today Abbie read us the story of Rapunzel, and then we looked at the letters **ou** and **ow**. Sometimes they make the same sounds.

Read this sentence and listen to the **ou** and **ow** sounds.

The princess was in a tall r**ou**nd t**ow**er.

Complete the words.

1

ow

<u>ow</u>l   c___   n___   h___   cr___n

Complete the words. Notice that **ou** never comes at the end of a word.

2

ou

c___nt   l___d   cl___d   f___nd   m___th

Now read all the words you made.

Let's practise

Make some new words. Write the new words you make. Read the words.

③   Change the **m** to **s** in **m**outh.   _south_

④   Change the **c** to **h** in **c**ow.

⑤   Change the **s** to **h** in **s**ound.

⑥   Change the **d** to **g** in **d**own.

⑦   Change the **m** to **h** in **m**ouse.

⑧   Change the **t** to **cr** in **t**own.

⑨   Change the **s** to **h** in **s**our.

⑩   Change the **fl** to **sh** in **fl**ower.

⑪   Change the **l** to **pr** in **l**oud.

⑫   Change the **cl** to **fr** in **cl**own.

Think of an **ou** word that rhymes with:

⑬   pound _____   loud _____   out _____

Now think of an **ow** word that rhymes with:

⑭   cow _____   down _____   tower _____

Teacher's tips

To find a word that rhymes, just change the first letter of the original word to a different consonant. Make sure your word is a real word and say it out loud to hear if it sounds right.

10: The *oi* and *oy* sounds

Today we're looking at **oi** and **oy**. Sometimes these letters sound the same. Let's read some words and listen for the **oi** and **oy** sounds.

That b**oy** has got a loud v**oi**ce!

Get ready

Read the words in the balloons.
Colour the **oi** balloons red.
Colour the **oy** balloons blue.

1

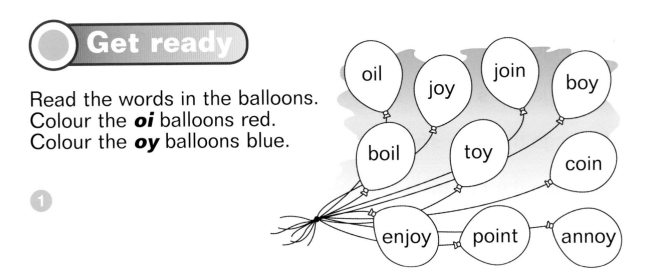

oil   joy   join   boy
boil   toy   coin
enjoy   point   annoy

Now write the words in sets.

2   **oi** words

3   **oy** words

Let's practise

Choose the correct **oi** word for each sentence.

> point　　boil　　voice　　join　　coin

4 　You ___ water in a kettle.

5 　You ___ wood together with a screw.

6 　You can buy things with a _____.

7 　You speak with your _____.

8 　You _____ with your finger.

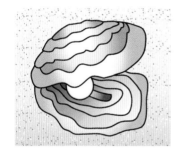

Now choose the correct **oy** word for each sentence.

> toy　　boy　　enjoy　　annoy　　oyster

9 　An _____ lives in the sea.

10 　I got a new _____ for my birthday.

11 　I _____ eating sweets.

12 　It is not nice to _____ other children.

13 　The _____ likes to play football.

Choose **oi** or **oy** to complete each word. Then colour the **oi** words red and the **oy** words blue.

14

___l	t___	sp___l	b___	n___se
h___st	ann___	m___st	destr___	r___al

Teacher's tips

Most of the time, the letter sound **oy** comes at the end of a word and the letter sound **oi** comes at the start or middle of a word but the words *oyster* and *royal* are exceptions!

11: The *or* and *aw* sounds

Abbie told us about the **or** and **aw** letters. They sometimes make the same sounds.

Read the words she showed us and listen to these sounds.

t*or*ch

s*aw*

Get ready

Complete the words. Write the words.

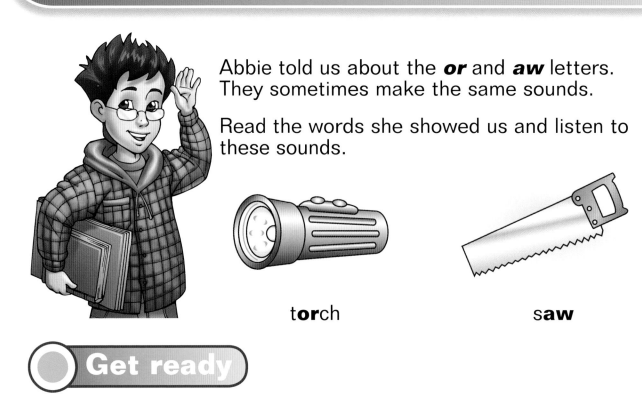

1. f_or_k   sh___t   h___n   st___m
   fork   _____   _____   _____

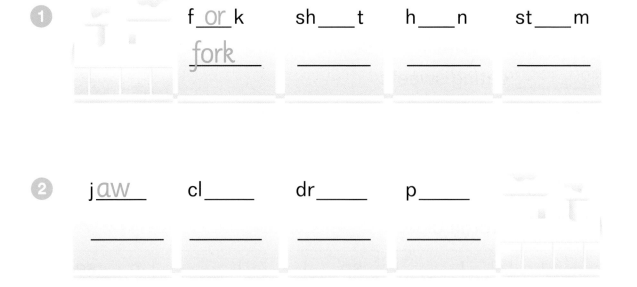

2. j_aw_   cl_____   dr_____   p_____
   _____   _____   _____   _____

Now read all the words you made.

Let's practise

Choose the correct word to answer the clues.

stork	crawl	torch	port	straw
cork	yawn	dawn	paws	thorn

3   This is in the top of a bottle.   _ _ _ _

4   A light   _ _ _ _ _

5   A cat has four of these.   _ _ _ _

6   A place for ships   _ _ _ _

7   You drink through this.   _ _ _ _ _

8   You can prick your finger on this.   _ _ _ _ _

9   The start of the day   _ _ _ _

10   A bird   _ _ _ _ _

11   You do this when you are tired.   _ _ _ _

12   Babies do this.   _ _ _ _ _

Write two words that end with:

aw	**awn**	**ork**	**ort**	**orn**

13   _____   _____   _____   _____   _____

     _____   _____   _____   _____   _____

Teacher's tips

For question 13, have your alphabet handy. Use it to help you go through all the consonant letter sounds until one of them sounds right and makes sense at the start of the other letters.

Today the boys have been collecting **ar** sounds and the girls have been collecting **ir** sounds. We've found lots of words with these sounds.

Can you find an **ir** sound and an **ar** sound in this sentence?

The g**ir**l is playing in the p**ar**k.

Get ready

Make the words. Write the words. Read the words.

1.
 c c ar   j c ar   s c t b ar

___car___   _____   _____

Label the pictures.

2.

___jar___   _____   _____

Make the words. Write the words. Read the words.

3.
b c ir b d   sh c ir b t   s c t b ir

_____   _____   _____

Let's practise

Choose the correct word. Write it under each picture.

4 card or cart?

cart

park or bark?

_____

arm or harm?

_____

tar or jar?

_____

5 shirt or skirt?

_____

first or thirst?

_____

girl or girder?

_____

thirty or thirsty?

_____

6 far or fir?

_____

star or stir?

_____

firm or farm?

_____

shirk or shark?

_____

Complete each word with **ar** or **ir**.

7 sk___t   t___   sc___f   ch___p   b___thday

p___ty   d___ty   g___den   m___k   g___l

Teacher's tips

Remember to read your words out loud in question 7. This might help you to spell the words and to spot any mistakes!

29

How have I done?

Complete the missing letters in each word.

1

f _ x   b _ d   h _ t   m _ _ g   t _ n

2

_ _ o p   _ _ e d   b a _ _

3

s o _ _   k i _ _   b e _ _

4

r _ _ d   t r _ _   s _ _

5

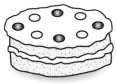 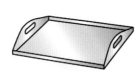 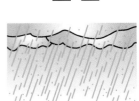

c _ k _   t r _ _   r _ _ n

6

f r _   k _ t _   n _ _ _ t

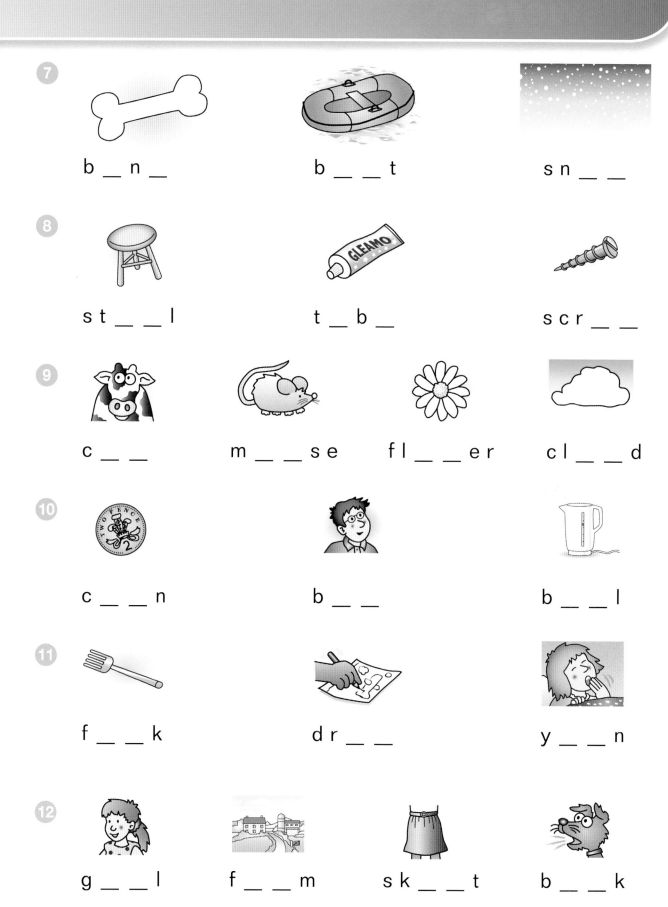

7

b _ n _

b _ _ t

s n _ _

8

s t _ _ l

t _ b _

s c r _ _

9

c _ _

m _ _ s e

f l _ _ e r

c l _ _ d

10

c _ _ n

b _ _

b _ _ l

11

f _ _ k

d r _ _

y _ _ n

12

g _ _ l

f _ _ m

s k _ _ t

b _ _ k

We hope you have enjoyed this visit to Kids Club. Come back and
see us soon!

Answers

UNIT 1
1 cat 2 red 3 pin 4 fox 5 mug 6 tin
7 jug 8 bed 9 hat 10 box
11 a hat on a rat; hat, rat
12 a ted on a bed; ted, bed
13 a tin on a bin; tin, bin
14 a dog on a log; dog, log
15 a mug on a rug; mug, rug
16 Many answers are possible. Accept any correct answers.

UNIT 2
1 chat chin chop chick
2 shop shed shut shell
3 thin thick think thank
4 bath, shed, fish, think
5 chop, chin, path, rich
6 brush, punch, dish, thief
7 and 8 Many answers are possible. Accept any correct answers.

UNIT 3
1 sock, king, bell
2 doll, tick, bang
3 king, bell, sock, bang, doll, tick
4 I fall off the wall.
   The king is on a swing.
5 A sock is on a rock.
   There is a bell on my shell.
6 I can sing a song.
   The sock is on the clock.
7 **ck** words – kick, lock, duck, back, peck
   ng words – wing, hang, long, thing, bring
   ll words – fill, yell, ball, well, till

UNIT 4
1 bee, sheep, need 2 three, green, week
3 eat, read, beach 4 sea, speak, clean
5 I can see a seal in the sea.
   There are three green apples in the tree.
6 I eat an ice cream on the beach.
   I need to go to sleep!
7 I sit on a seat and read a book.
   I sweep my room and make it clean.

ee words – see, three, green, tree, need, sleep, sweep
ea words – seal, sea, eat, cream, beach, seat, read, clean

8 weep, meal, teach, steep, keep, neat
   beak, peep, feel, mean, each, cheek

UNIT 5
1 day, say, pay, play, clay
2 train, paint, nail, tail, afraid
3 On Sunday I went out to play.
4 On Monday I went on a boat with a sail.
5 On Tuesday I made a pot with clay.
6 On Wednesday I saw a rat with a long tail.
7 On Thursday I went for a swim in the bay.
8 On Friday I got a hammer and hit a nail.
9 hate, cape, made, tape, cane

UNIT 6
1 cry fly fry
2 fry cry fly
3 light night fight
4 try, tight, shy, right, dry, might, sight or sigh, why, bright or right
5 pip, rip, win, pin, spin

UNIT 7
1 low blow slow show grow
2 coat road loaf soap moan
3 mow 4 slow 5 show
6 crow 7 shadow 8 boat – goat
9 cloak – soak 10 moan – groan 11 road – toad
12 toast – roast
13 hope, robe, note, slope, mope

UNIT 8
1 zoo, pool, roof 2 moon, boot, room
3 new, few, chew 4 stew, drew, flew
5 moon, new, chew, boot, broom
6 stew, screw, school, stool, threw
7 threw, broom, moon, chew, stew
8 screw, school, stool, new, boot
9 cub, us, tub, cut, plum

UNIT 9
1 owl, cow, now, how, crown
2 count, loud, cloud, found, mouth
3 south 4 how 5 hound 6 gown 7 house
8 crown 9 hour 10 shower 11 proud 12 frown
13 and 14 Many answers are possible. Accept any correct answers.

UNIT 10
1 red **oi** words – oil, boil, join, point, coin
   blue **oy** words – toy, boy, joy, enjoy, annoy
2 **oi** words – oil, boil, join, point, coin
3 **oy** words – toy, boy, joy, enjoy, annoy
4 You boil water in a kettle.
5 You join wood together with a screw.
6 You can buy things with a coin.
7 You speak with your voice.
8 You point with your finger.
9 An oyster lives in the sea.
10 I got a new toy for my birthday.
11 I enjoy eating sweets.
12 It is not nice to annoy other children.
13 The boy likes to play football.
14 oil, toy, spoil, boy, noise / hoist, annoy, moist, destroy, royal
   blue **oy** words – toy, boy, annoy, destroy, royal
   red **oi** words – oil, spoil, noise, hoist, moist

UNIT 11
1 fork short horn storm
2 jaw claw draw paw
3 cork 4 torch 5 paws 6 port 7 straw
8 thorn 9 dawn 10 stork 11 yawn 12 crawl
13 Many answers are possible. Accept any correct answers.

UNIT 12
1 car, jar, star 2 jar, star, car
3 bird, shirt, stir 4 cart, bark, arm, jar
5 skirt, first, girl, thirty 6 fir, star, farm, shark
7 skirt, tar, scarf, chirp, birthday / party, dirty, garden, mark, girl

HOW HAVE I DONE?
1 fox, bed, hat, mug, tin 2 chop, shed, bath
3 sock, king, bell 4 read, tree, sea
5 cake, tray, rain 6 fry, kite, night
7 bone, boat, snow 8 stool, tube, screw
9 cow, mouse, flower, cloud 10 coin, boy, boil
11 fork, draw, yawn 12 girl, farm, skirt, bark